Casey Means Biography:

How Dr. Casey Means is Revolutionizing Health and Wellness

Fabulous Press

Copyright

Table of Contents

Introduction:

A Promise to Our Readers

This book is more than just Dr. Means' biography; it's a manifesto for change in the face of modern health crises. By the end of this book, you won't just be moved; you'll be motivated to take control of your health and equipped to make lasting changes. Expect to close this book with a new perspective on health and a renewed vigor to act on it.

Welcome to a Revelation in Health and Wellness

Embark on an unprecedented journey with Dr. Casey Means, a visionary who is not just changing the landscape of healthcare but revolutionizing our everyday lives. This isn't just another biography; it's your personal gateway to transforming how you think about health, technology, and the power of preventive medicine. Dr. Means isn't just a doctor; she's a catalyst for global change.

Why This Book Will Change Your Life

While many books offer insights, this biography provides a blueprint for a healthier, more vibrant life. Each page sparks a revolution in your understanding of your body's potential. This isn't just Dr. Means' story; it's the future of your wellness journey. Here's what you'll gain:

- **Empowerment Through Education:** Learn how your daily choices can dramatically alter your health and well-being.
- **Technological Transformation:** Discover the cutting-edge tools that can monitor and manage your metabolic health.
- **Dietary Revolution:** Explore how plant-based nutrition can restore and rejuvenate your body at a cellular level.

Exclusive Bonuses Just for Readers

- **Step-by-Step Guides to Metabolic Health**: Practical tools to implement the Levels approach in your daily life.
- **Personal Wellness Plans:** Tailored advice from Dr. Means that readers can start using today to improve their health.

Chapter 1: A Mind Ignited

Beyond Genius: The Early Spark of a Future Health Revolutionary.

In the heart of the lush Pacific Northwest, where the rain often plays its gentle symphony on the verdant landscapes, a young Casey Means would stare out of the window, her mind buzzing with questions that stretched far beyond the classroom discussions on biology and human anatomy. It was here, amid the rolling hills and towering evergreens of Portland, Oregon, that the early sparks of a future health revolutionary were ignited.

From a tender age, Casey exhibited an insatiable curiosity about the natural world and a profound compassion for living beings. Her parents, both educators, recognized and nurtured her budding potential, providing her with books that opened new realms of knowledge and wisdom. They taught her that learning was not just an academic exercise, but a doorway to influence the world positively. "Knowledge," her father would often say, "is the most potent tool we have to change the world."

Casey's educational journey was punctuated with accolades, but her quest was never about the accolades themselves. She was driven by an unyielding desire to understand how things worked—particularly, how the human body worked. She devoured texts on physiology and biochemistry, not just to ace her exams, but to piece together the puzzles of human health. This relentless pursuit of knowledge led her to Stanford University, a place that promised more than just an education—it offered an opportunity to truly make a difference.

At Stanford, Casey's passion for health took a definitive shape. Surrounded by some of the brightest minds in medicine and technology, she began to see the vast possibilities of integrating these fields to pioneer preventive healthcare solutions. Her days and nights blurred into a continuous loop of classes, lab sessions, and endless discussions with professors and peers about the future of medicine. It was during one of these discussions that she encountered a quote by Hippocrates that would forever shape her career: "Let food be thy medicine and medicine be thy food."

This simple yet profound statement became the cornerstone of Casey's philosophy. It wasn't enough to treat symptoms; she wanted to prevent them. She envisioned a world where chronic diseases were not just managed but prevented through lifestyle choices and technological innovation. Her commitment to this vision was palpable, earning her the respect of her professors and the admiration of her peers.

The turning point came when she attended a conference on metabolic health. Here, she learned about the burgeoning field of continuous glucose monitoring (CGM) technology. The potential of CGM to provide real-time insights into how dietary choices affect glucose levels struck a chord with her. She realized that this technology could be a key to unlocking personalized nutrition—a way to show individuals, in undeniable data, how their bodies react to what they eat.

Emboldened by this revelation, Casey began to work on a project that combined CGM with a mobile app to provide users with actionable health insights. The project was ambitious and fraught with challenges, from technical hurdles to skepticism from traditionalists in the medical field. But Casey was undeterred. "Innovation," she asserted, "is not just about having new ideas; it's about making new ideas happen."

Her resolve paid off when she met like-minded entrepreneurs who shared her vision. Together, they founded Levels, a company that would go on to revolutionize the way people understand and manage their metabolic health. Under her leadership, Levels became more than just a tech company; it became a movement, empowering individuals to take control of their health destiny.

Casey's journey from a curious child in Portland to a health tech visionary was not just a tale of personal success; it was a testament to the power of education, passion, and perseverance. Her story is a beacon for anyone who dreams of making a difference, proving that with the right amount of knowledge, conviction, and courage, changing the world is not just possible—it's inevitable.

Chapter 2: From Scalpels to Silicon

A Daring Leap from Operating Rooms to Startup Dreams, Charting the Pivotal Moments that Redirected Her Life's Mission

In the sterile silence of the operating room, where life and science intersect with razor-sharp precision, Dr. Casey Means found her calling. She was a rising star in the world of otolaryngology, gifted with a surgeon's hands and a healer's heart. Yet, as she stood over the operating table day after day, a nagging question began to echo in her mind: "Am I really making the most profound impact possible?"

This question haunted her, lingering in the corners of her mind as she performed surgeries that, while lifesaving, often felt like they were merely addressing the symptoms of deeper, preventable health issues. It was during these reflective moments that Casey encountered a quote by Albert Einstein that struck a profound chord: "Intellectuals solve problems, geniuses prevent them."

Driven by this new perspective, Casey began to reevaluate her path. She knew she had more to offer the world than her surgical skills; she wanted to prevent the diseases she was treating. This realization came sharply into focus when she attended a seminar on the burgeoning field of health technology. Here, she saw the potential to leverage technology not just to treat but to transform and prevent chronic health issues.

The seminar was a revelation. It showcased startups working on innovative health solutions, from apps that tracked mental health to devices that monitored chronic diseases. The energy was electric, charged with ideas and possibilities that bridged technology and wellness in ways Casey had only dreamed of. It was here that she encountered another pivotal quote by Steve

Jobs: *"Innovation distinguishes between a leader and a follower."*

Casey decided she didn't just want to follow paths; she wanted to pave them. She envisioned a platform that could integrate the emerging technology of continuous glucose monitoring with a user-friendly interface to help people understand and optimize their metabolic health. The idea was revolutionary and filled her with a purpose that surgery no longer provided.

Making the decision to leave her surgical career was not easy. It meant stepping away from a prestigious and secure position into the uncertain world of startups. It was a risk that many of her colleagues questioned and few understood. But for Casey, the risk was not just about changing careers; it was about answering a higher calling.

She often recalled the words of T.S. Eliot during this transitional phase: "Only those who will risk going too far can possibly find out how far one can go." It was with this spirit that she embraced her next challenge—co-founding Levels. The startup was more than just a business venture; it was the embodiment of her mission to transform healthcare from reactive to proactive.

The early days of Levels were filled with challenges. Casey and her team faced skepticism from traditional medical practitioners and struggled to secure funding from investors who failed to see the potential of preventive health technology. Despite these hurdles, Casey's conviction did not waver. She believed in the power of data to empower individuals and in the importance of metabolic health as the foundation of overall wellness.

Her belief was contagious, gradually attracting a team of like-minded innovators, securing the necessary funding, and building a community of early adopters who shared her vision. Each milestone was a validation of her decision to pivot from scalpel to silicon, from treating symptoms to preventing them.

Casey's journey is a testament to the power of daring to dream differently. Her leap from the operating room to the boardroom was not just a career change but a redefinition of what it means to be a doctor. She didn't abandon her oath to save lives; she expanded it to save more lives than she ever could have one surgery at a time.

In Casey's words: *"The greatest risk is not taking one."* This chapter closes with an invitation to you: to think bigger, to act bolder, and to imagine a world where health is not just treated but cherished and preserved.

Chapter 3: The Levels Legacy Begins

The Birth of a Breakthrough: How a Simple Idea Grew into a Movement that Redefined Health Metrics

In the bustling heart of Silicon Valley, where ideas soar as high as the aspirations of those who dare to dream, Dr. Casey Means planted the seeds of what would soon become a revolutionary shift in health metrics. The concept was elegantly simple yet profoundly impactful: to harness the power of continuous glucose monitoring (CGM) technology to revolutionize personal health management.

This chapter of Dr. Means' journey begins not in a laboratory or a boardroom, but in a quiet, reflective moment. While reading a research paper on the metabolic patterns of diabetes patients, she was struck by a staggering realization: the principles of glucose monitoring could be applied universally, not just for diabetes management but for optimizing the health of the entire population. It was a eureka moment, underscored by the words of Marie Curie that she had once noted in her journal: "Be less curious about people and more curious about ideas."

With this spark, the idea for Levels was born—a platform that would make metabolic health accessible and understandable for everyone. Dr. Means envisioned a tool that could provide real-time feedback on how different foods affected an individual's body, turning abstract nutrition advice into personalized, actionable data.

She began assembling a team, pulling together experts in medicine, technology, and data science. Each team member was chosen not only for their expertise but for their passion for changing the world. Together, they shared a belief that Thomas Edison once eloquently expressed: "The value of an idea lies in the using of it."

In the early stages, the team faced significant challenges. The first was the technological hurdle of adapting medical-grade CGM technology for everyday consumer use. They needed to ensure it was not only accurate but also user-friendly and affordable. Many late nights were spent in brainstorming sessions, with whiteboards filled with diagrams and equations, as they pushed the boundaries of what was possible.

The second challenge was societal acceptance. They needed to shift public perception—educating people on the importance of metabolic health and overcoming the stigma often associated with medical devices. Dr. Means took a proactive approach, launching educational campaigns and speaking at health and wellness conferences. She articulated the vision of Levels with such clarity and passion that it resonated deeply with her audiences. Her favorite quote by William James often echoed in these halls: *"Act as if what you do makes a difference. It does."*

As Levels launched its beta program, the initial feedback was overwhelmingly positive. Early users reported not only improvements in their dietary choices but profound insights into how their bodies responded to different types of food. What was once invisible—the fluctuating levels of glucose in one's bloodstream—was now visible, and knowledge became power.

The media began to take notice, and soon Levels was not just a product but a movement. Stories poured in from users who had transformed their lives using the insights from their CGM data. Each testimonial was a ripple in the pond of the healthcare industry, spreading wider and gaining momentum.

The real breakthrough came when a renowned health influencer documented her journey with Levels on social media. Her story of transformation—backed by the hard data from her own CGM—captivated millions. It was not just about losing weight or managing a condition; it was about reclaiming control over one's health and vitality. It underscored Dr. Means' belief that "empowerment begins with understanding."

As this chapter closes, you are left with a vivid picture of how a simple idea, rooted in the desire to empower individuals with knowledge, grew into a movement that redefined health metrics. Dr. Means' journey with Levels is more than a success story—it's a call to action for you, to embrace the power of technology to enhance your health and to be proactive stewards of your well-being.

Through Levels, Dr. Casey Means not only changed how people viewed their dietary choices but fundamentally shifted the dialogue around health care from reactive to proactive. She proved that with the right tools and information, anyone could become the architect of their own health destiny.

Chapter 4: Sugar, We're Going Down

Unveiling the Bitter Truths About Sugar and Dr. Means' Crusade Against the Hidden Enemy in Our Diet

In a world sweetened by hidden sugars, Dr. Casey Means embarked on a formidable crusade to reveal the bitter truths lurking in our everyday meals. With the precision of a scientist and the passion of a reformer, she set out to expose sugar not just as a dietary component but as a pervasive threat to global health.

Dr. Means' journey into the sugar battleground began with a startling revelation from a comprehensive study: the average American was consuming more than triple the daily recommended amount of sugar. This overconsumption was not just a pathway to obesity but a contributor to a litany of health issues like diabetes, heart disease, and metabolic dysfunction. Armed with this knowledge, Dr. Means likened sugar to a "silent killer," an adversary worthy of public enemy status.

Inspired by the urgency of this health crisis, Dr. Means took to the public stage, leveraging every platform from academic symposiums to social media to educate the public. She drew upon a poignant quote from Hippocrates that she often cited: "Let food be thy medicine and medicine be thy food," using it to underline the detrimental effects of sugar as anti-medicine, a substance that corrupts rather than cures.

At Levels, Dr. Means spearheaded the development of educational programs that not only highlighted the dangers of sugar but also taught people how to detect and reduce it in their diet. The company's app included features that tracked sugar intake and provided feedback on how to optimize one's diet for better health. Each feature was crafted with the user in mind, turning complex data into simple, actionable advice.

The centerpiece of her anti-sugar campaign was the "Sugar Reset Challenge," a program designed to help individuals experience firsthand the impact of reducing sugar intake. Participants were equipped with continuous glucose monitors and guided through a month of dietary adjustments. The results were eye-opening: many reported not only weight loss but also enhanced energy levels, improved sleep quality, and a decrease in cravings.

Dr. Means' message resonated deeply, touching a nerve in a society that was waking up to the realities of dietary negligence. Her talks often featured a powerful visual—a jar filled with the amount of sugar consumed annually by the average person, a stark illustration that left audiences both shocked and motivated.

Her crusade was not without its detractors. The sugar industry, armed with its own set of researchers and marketing mavens, launched counter-campaigns to downplay the risks associated with sugar consumption. But Dr. Means was undeterred, often quoting Margaret Mead in her presentations: "Never doubt that a small group of thoughtful, committed citizens can change the world; indeed, it's the only thing that ever has."

As the movement grew, stories of transformation emerged. There was the tale of a young mother who, after participating in the Sugar Reset Challenge, was able to wean herself off insulin for her type 2 diabetes, and a teenager who overcame his chronic acne issues by cutting out sugar. Each story added a human face to the statistics, making the cause not just compelling but personal.

Dr. Means also pushed for policy changes, advocating for clearer labeling on food products and stricter regulations on marketed children's foods. She envisioned a future where sugar's presence was not hidden behind confusing labels but transparent, allowing consumers to make more informed choices about their health.

As this chapter concludes, you are left with a profound understanding of the insidious nature of sugar and the transformative power of awareness and action. Dr. Means' battle against sugar is depicted not just as a personal mission but as a global imperative, a call to arms for anyone who values their health and the health of future generations. Through her relentless advocacy and innovative approaches, she not only illuminates the path to better health but inspires a movement that dares to confront one of the modern diet's most dangerous culprits.

Chapter 5: The Green Revolution

How a Doctor's Personal Vegan Journey is
Transforming the Plate of the Nation

In a narrative that is as green and vibrant as
the food she champions, Dr. Casey Means'
journey into veganism is not just a personal
choice, but a profound transformation that is
reshaping the dietary landscape of a nation.
From the lush, fertile valleys of personal
health to the sprawling urban expanses of
public nutritional reform, her story is a
testament to the power of plant-based eating.

Dr. Means' vegan voyage began not in the
kitchen, but in the laboratory, where her deep
dive into metabolic health research revealed
startling connections between dietary choices
and chronic diseases. It was here, among petri
dishes and medical journals, that she

encountered a compelling quote by Thomas Edison: "The doctor of the future will no longer treat the human frame with drugs, but rather will cure and prevent disease with nutrition." This insight struck a chord with her, sowing the seeds for her green revolution.

Transitioning to a vegan diet, Dr. Means experienced firsthand the profound impact of plant-based nutrition. She noted significant improvements in her energy levels, cognitive clarity, and overall well-being. These personal benefits, coupled with the scientific research supporting plant-based diets' role in reducing the risk of major health issues like heart disease, diabetes, and obesity, solidified her commitment to advocate for dietary change.

Dr. Means began to share her journey and the benefits of a vegan diet through public speaking engagements, social media, and at medical conferences, where she presented compelling data and personal anecdotes to inspire her colleagues and the public. Her message was clear and potent: "Change your diet, change your life, change the world."

At Levels, she integrated plant-based dietary guidance into the app, providing users with not just data on their metabolic health, but also actionable insights on how to incorporate more plant-based foods into their diets. The app featured recipes, meal plans, and nutritional information designed to ease the transition to a vegan lifestyle, thus democratizing health one plate at a time.

Her influence extended beyond the digital world. Dr. Means collaborated with schools, community centers, and local governments to promote urban agriculture projects and plant-based school lunch programs. She envisioned cities where fresh produce was as accessible as fast food, and children grew up knowing the taste of fresh vegetables straight from the garden.

The impact of her work was palpable. Stories began to emerge from individuals and families whose lives had been transformed by the switch to a vegan diet. There was the story of a father who reversed his heart disease, a young woman who overcame her struggle with obesity, and an elderly couple who found new vitality in their golden years—all united by the changes advocated by Dr. Means.

However, her green revolution was not without challenges. The meat and dairy industries pushed back, armed with their own studies and media campaigns. But Dr. Means was undeterred, often quoting Ralph Waldo Emerson in her rebuttals: "To be yourself in a world that is constantly trying to make you something else is the greatest accomplishment."

As this chapter draws to a close, you are not just inspired by Dr. Means' journey but also equipped with the knowledge and tools to embark on their own plant-based adventures. Her story is more than a narrative about dietary change; it's a rallying cry for environmental stewardship, public health, and compassionate living.

Through Dr. Casey Means' eyes, we see a world where the health of individuals and the planet are intertwined, where every meal is an opportunity for wellness and sustainability. Her revolution is not waged with force, but with forks—a green revolution that invites us all to the table to partake in the bounty of the Earth, to heal ourselves and our world one meal at a time.

Chapter 6: Echoes of Change

How Dr. Means' Voice is Shaping the Future of Health, One Podcast, One Talk, One Tweet at a Time

In a world awash with information yet starving for wisdom, Dr. Casey Means has emerged as a guiding light, her voice a clarion call to action in the realm of health. Harnessing the pervasive power of modern communication—from podcasts and public speeches to tweets and Instagram posts—Dr. Means is not just participating in the conversation; she is leading it.

Dr. Means understands that in the digital age, influence is no longer confined to the halls of universities or the pages of medical journals. It flows through the airwaves, across the internet, and into the devices that populate every corner of our lives. With this understanding, she embarked on a mission to make health knowledge accessible, engaging, and, most importantly, actionable.

Her foray into the world of digital communication began with a simple podcast. Sitting in a makeshift studio—little more than a quiet room and a microphone—she recorded her first episode. It was a deep dive into metabolic health, a topic she could discuss with the ease most people reserve for chatting about the weather. The podcast was an instant hit, resonating with listeners hungry for insights on how to take control of their health through informed choices.

With each episode, Dr. Means explored topics ranging from the science of glucose monitoring to the benefits of anti-inflammatory foods, always linking back to how these elements play pivotal roles in overall wellness. She often quoted Leonardo da Vinci, saying, "Learning never exhausts the mind," a mantra that echoed through her episodes and encouraged continuous curiosity among her audience.

Her impact grew exponentially as she took to the stage at various health and wellness conferences. Here, she spoke not just to rooms but to thousands around the world via live streams. Her speeches were masterclasses in the intersection of technology and health, filled with compelling data, personal anecdotes, and a vision for a future where everyone could be the steward of their own health. One of her most quoted lines, "Empowerment through education," became a rallying cry for her followers.

Dr. Means' social media platforms became extensions of her mission. Each tweet, each Instagram post, was meticulously crafted to educate, inspire, and provoke thought. When she shared a graph showing the impact of a single processed meal on blood sugar levels, it went viral, sparking discussions in online forums and dinner tables alike. She used these tools not just to inform but to challenge societal norms about eating and health.

But perhaps the most significant of her platforms was her YouTube channel, where she hosted live Q&A sessions, debunking myths and sharing the latest research in metabolic health. These sessions made her not just a voice but a presence in people's lives, providing direct, personal engagement with her audience. She often reminded her viewers, "Ask questions, seek truth," urging them to be active participants in their health journeys.

Her influence was also felt in academia and policy-making. As her reputation grew, policymakers invited her to consult on public health initiatives, recognizing that her insights could help shape better health outcomes on a national scale. Her advocacy for better food labeling and access to preventive health tools began to find echoes in legislation, showing that her words had power beyond the digital realm.

Dr. Means' reach and impact are a testament to her understanding of the dynamics of modern communication. She knows that to change the world, one must speak to it in its own language, and today, that language is digital. Each podcast, talk, tweet, and post is a pebble thrown into the vast ocean of public discourse, creating ripples that spread and multiply in ways that are both seen and unseen.

As you turn the final page of this chapter, you are not just reading about a medical professional using her voice; you've witnessed a leader crafting a new paradigm for health communication. Dr. Means' story inspires not just because of what she says, but because of how she says it—with clarity, passion, and unwavering commitment to the truth. Her voice, echoing across platforms and continents, continues to inspire a health revolution, one listener, one viewer, one follower at a time.

Chapter 7: The Wellness Warrior's Toolkit

Inside Dr. Means' Personal and Professional Regimen that Fuels Her Fight for a Healthier World

In a world increasingly burdened by health crises, Dr. Casey Means stands as a beacon of vitality and vision. Her daily regimen is not just a routine but a ritual, a meticulously crafted arsenal of habits, tools, and philosophies that empower her to lead a global health revolution. This chapter delves deep into the personal and professional life of Dr. Means, revealing the secrets behind her boundless energy and relentless drive.

Dr. Means starts her day before sunrise, believing in Benjamin Franklin's wisdom, "Early to bed and early to rise, makes a man healthy, wealthy, and wise." Her mornings begin with a moment of stillness, meditating in the quiet predawn hours to clear her mind and center her thoughts. Meditation, for Dr. Means, is more than relaxation; it's a tool for cultivating mental clarity and resilience, essential for anyone navigating the complexities of modern healthcare.

Following meditation, Dr. Means engages in a physical workout that is both rigorous and rejuvenating. She alternates between yoga, to enhance flexibility and balance, and high-intensity interval training (HIIT) to boost her cardiovascular health and metabolic efficiency. This physical conditioning is complemented by a breakfast that is as nutritious as it is delicious—a smoothie made from kale, berries, flax seeds, and almond milk, packed with antioxidants, vitamins, and minerals that fuel her body for the challenges ahead.

Her professional toolkit is equally robust, featuring a blend of cutting-edge technology and time-tested wisdom. At the heart of her toolkit is the continuous glucose monitor

(CGM), a device that not only guides her dietary choices but also serves as a cornerstone of her health tech company, Levels. This device provides real-time feedback on her metabolic responses, enabling her to fine-tune her diet based on scientific data rather than guesswork.

Dr. Means is a staunch advocate for what she calls "data-driven living," a philosophy where decisions about diet, exercise, and wellness are based on personalized health data. This approach is reflected in her use of various health apps that track everything from her sleep patterns to her heart rate variability, tools that allow her to maintain optimal health amidst her busy schedule.

Her professional regimen also includes a rigorous review of the latest research in metabolic health, which she integrates into her work and public engagements. Dr. Means is committed to lifelong learning, often quoting Michelangelo, "I am still learning," to remind her team and her audience that education is a continuous journey, not a destination.

Nutrition plays a pivotal role in Dr. Means' wellness toolkit. As a vegan, she chooses foods that reduce inflammation and boost cognitive function, such as avocados, nuts, and whole grains. Her diet is carefully planned to include all essential nutrients, proving that one can thrive on a plant-based regimen.

Community engagement is another critical component of her toolkit. Dr. Means frequently hosts webinars and workshops, not only to educate but also to listen and learn from others' experiences. These interactions provide her with insights into the real-world impacts of her work and fuel her motivation to continue her advocacy.

Dr. Means also emphasizes the importance of mental health, incorporating regular "digital detoxes" to reduce stress and prevent burnout. She believes in nurturing the mind as diligently as the body, adhering to the adage, "A sound mind in a sound body," as she balances her professional obligations with personal growth and relaxation.

As this chapter concludes, you are left with a comprehensive portrait of a woman whose life is as disciplined as it is passionate. Dr. Means' regimen is a testament to her commitment not just to her own health but to the health of the planet. Her toolkit, rich with technological innovation, physical wellness practices, and a deep connection to community, is not just for personal benefit but serves as a model for anyone seeking to make a difference in the world.

Through Dr. Means' example, you are invited to consider how your own daily habits can contribute to their goals and ideals. This chapter not only inspires but also challenges each of us to build our own wellness toolkit, crafting a life of health, wisdom, and profound impact.

Chapter 8: Heartbeats and Bits

The Synergy of Technology and Human Touch in Medicine—Personal Stories of Lives Touched and Transformed

In an era where technology increasingly interfaces with every aspect of human life, Dr. Casey Means stands at the forefront, pioneering a movement where technology and human touch do not just coexist but synergize to transform medicine. This chapter delves into the profound impacts of this integration, told through the personal stories of individuals whose lives have been dramatically changed by Dr. Means' vision.

The narrative begins with a poignant account of Tom, a middle-aged truck driver with a history of type 2 diabetes and heart disease, emblematic of millions struggling under the burden of chronic illness. Tom's journey with Dr. Means' technology started with a small, wearable device—a continuous glucose monitor (CGM) that Levels made accessible beyond the confines of the medical community. For the first time in his life, Tom could see in real-time how his dietary choices affected his blood sugar levels. Empowered by this data, he made small but significant changes that cumulated in a major reduction in his diabetic symptoms and medication dependency. "Every human being is the author of his own health or disease," Dr. Means often quotes from Buddha, underscoring her belief in empowering individuals through technology.

Next, the chapter introduces us to Sarah, a high school teacher who suffered from chronic fatigue and stress, common ailments in today's fast-paced world. Sarah's encounter with Dr. Means' holistic health app, which integrates meditation and mindfulness practices alongside physical health tracking, provided her with a toolkit to manage her stress and improve her energy levels. The app's personalized insights guided Sarah to a balanced lifestyle that improved both her mental and physical well-being, illustrating Dr. Means' conviction that "health is a state of complete harmony of the body, mind, and spirit."

The stories then shift to the global stage, highlighting Dr. Means' collaboration with healthcare providers in under-resourced communities. In a small village in India, a pilot program utilizing mobile health technology provided prenatal care advice and monitoring through smartphones. This program significantly reduced complications during childbirth and improved outcomes for mothers and babies, showcasing the scalability and impact of Dr. Means' technologies. Through these efforts, Dr. Means demonstrates the truth of her guiding principle: "Technology is nothing without the people it serves."

Each story is woven with the theme of connection—not just the wireless connections of devices, but the human connections that these technologies facilitate. Dr. Means believes in technology as a bridge, not a barrier, enhancing the doctor-patient relationship, enabling personalized care, and creating communities of health. She often quotes Steve Jobs, who said, "Technology is best when it brings people together."

The chapter also explores the ethical dimensions and challenges of integrating technology in healthcare, discussing privacy concerns, the digital divide, and the potential for depersonalization. Dr. Means addresses these issues head-on, advocating for responsible innovation that prioritizes patient welfare and inclusivity. Her approach is not to overshadow the human element of medicine but to amplify it through technology that listens, learns, and adapts to individual needs.

As the chapter closes, you are left with a deeper understanding of how Dr. Means' work is not merely about deploying cutting-edge gadgets but about re-envisioning what healthcare can look like when technology and compassion converge. It is a vision beautifully encapsulated in her favorite quote from Albert Schweitzer: *"The purpose of human life is to serve, and to show compassion and the will to help others."*

Through the lens of technology, Dr. Means not only touches hearts but also saves lives, proving that in the right hands, bits and heartbeats can together sing a harmonious symphony of health and humanity.

Chapter 9: The Feminine Force in Tech

Shattering Glass Ceilings: The Triumphs and Trials of a Woman Reshaping the Male-Dominated Tech Landscape

In the ever-evolving, fast-paced world of technology, Dr. Casey Means stands out not just for her innovative contributions but as a beacon of inspiration for women everywhere. Battling the stereotypical norms and entrenched gender biases of Silicon Valley, she has forged a path laden with both significant achievements and formidable challenges. This chapter unfolds the inspiring journey of Dr. Means as she shatters glass ceilings and reshapes the male-dominated tech landscape, transforming adversity into opportunity.

The narrative begins with Dr. Means at a tech conference, the only woman on a panel of men. As she shares her vision for integrating health technology with preventive medicine, her voice is firm, her data compelling, and her presence undeniable. Despite the initial underestimation by some peers, her session ends with a standing ovation—a testament to her expertise and passion. This moment echoes Madeleine Albright's words, which Dr. Means often quotes: "It took me quite a long time to develop a voice, and now that I have it, I am not going to be silent."

Dr. Means' journey into the tech world was met with a mixture of skepticism and intrigue. As she ventured into the development of Levels, her startup that combines continuous glucose monitoring with user-friendly software, she faced the dual challenges of pioneering a new concept and proving her worth in a field where women are often overlooked. Each investor meeting tested her resolve, but she armed herself with undeniable data and a clear vision, gradually turning skepticism into investment and doubt into belief.

However, the challenges were manifold. She encountered venture capitalists who questioned her capacity to lead a tech startup due to her medical background and gender. Each instance was a stark reminder of the biases that still permeate the tech industry. Dr. Means, however, saw these challenges not as barriers but as motivations to push harder. She often reflects on the words of Michelle Obama, "There is no limit to what we, as women, can accomplish," using them as a mantra to fuel her determination.

The chapter also highlights Dr. Means' role as a mentor to young women entering the tech field. Through initiatives like coding workshops for girls and mentorship programs, she provides the guidance and encouragement that were scarce when she was climbing the ranks. Her efforts have not only helped to pave the way for the next generation of female tech leaders but also cultivated a community that supports and uplifts one another.

Dr. Means' influence extends beyond business success; she actively participates in forums and panels discussing diversity in tech, using her platform to advocate for systemic change. Her talks often include discussions on the importance of creating inclusive work environments that value and nurture diversity, echoing the sentiment of Ruth Bader Ginsburg, "Women belong in all places where decisions are being made."

Amidst the trials, Dr. Means' triumphs continue to accumulate. Levels has grown into a formidable presence in the tech world, with its success serving as a case study in several business schools. Dr. Means has also been featured on lists of top women in tech, recognized not just for her business acumen but for her role in breaking down gender barriers in the technology sector.

As the chapter concludes, readers are left with a vivid portrayal of a woman who is not only reshaping the tech landscape but also redefining what it means to be a leader in technology. Dr. Means' story is a compelling reminder of the power of resilience, the importance of mentorship, and the transformative impact of having a voice in a world that often tries to silence it.

Through her journey, Dr. Casey Means does more than innovate; she inspires, making every challenge a stepping stone and every achievement a beacon for those who will follow. Her path is a testament to the strength and potential of the feminine force in technology, proving that with courage, conviction, and compassion, even the toughest glass ceilings can be shattered.

Chapter 10: The Global Glucose Guardian

From Silicon Valley to Global Villages: How Dr. Means' Vision is Reaching Underserved Populations

In the heart of Silicon Valley, a place known for its cutting-edge innovation and staggering wealth, Dr. Casey Means has embarked on a mission that stretches far beyond the tech-savvy elite, reaching into the corners of the earth where healthcare is not a service but a struggle. This chapter tells the compelling story of how Dr. Means' groundbreaking work in metabolic health is transforming lives in underserved populations, making her a guardian not just of glucose but of global well-being.

Dr. Means' journey as the Global Glucose Guardian began when she recognized the universal challenge of metabolic diseases, which know no borders. Her realization that "health is a universal language" steered her vision towards global health equity, a commitment to ensure that everyone, regardless of their geographical or economic circumstances, has access to the tools they need to manage their health.

The narrative unfolds with the introduction of a pilot program in rural India, where diabetes rates are soaring, yet diagnostic tools are scarce. Partnering with local health workers, Dr. Means helped to distribute portable, easy-to-use glucose monitors that could function effectively in low-resource settings. This initiative not only provided much-needed data on the community's metabolic health but also empowered individuals with knowledge previously inaccessible to them.

Dr. Means' approach was simple yet profound: equip people with the tools to see the invisible, and you empower them to make visible changes. She often cites a powerful quote that fuels her mission: "Give a man a fish, and you feed him for a day. Teach a man to fish, and you feed him for a lifetime." By providing communities with glucose monitors, she was teaching them to fish in the vast ocean of health management.

The impact of this initiative was heartwarming and significant. The chapter shares the story of Anjali, a young mother in the village who learned to manage her gestational diabetes through the program. Anjali's experience highlighted the transformative power of accessible health technology—her healthy delivery and the birth of her thriving baby became a beacon of hope and a testament to the program's success.

Expanding from India to sub-Saharan Africa, Dr. Means introduced mobile clinics that brought glucose monitoring and health education directly to remote villages. These mobile clinics were equipped with solar-powered devices, ensuring they could operate independently of the unreliable local power grid. The clinics not only conducted health screenings but also hosted educational workshops where villagers learned about nutrition, exercise, and the importance of regular health monitoring.

Dr. Means' work also addressed the educational gap by providing online resources available in multiple languages, accessible via smartphones. This digital outreach helped bridge the divide between urban and rural, rich and poor, educated and unlearned. Each online session, each piece of downloadable content, was a step towards democratizing health knowledge.

In her speeches, Dr. Means emphasizes the importance of empathy and innovation in tackling global health challenges. She inspires her audience with stories from the field, reminding them that "Technology is the tool, but compassion is the catalyst." It is this blend of high-tech solutions and high-touch approaches that has marked her efforts with success.

As the chapter closes, you are left inspired by Dr. Means' unwavering commitment to global health equity. Her work is not just about distributing technology but about fostering a worldwide community where every individual has the chance to lead a healthier life. Through her initiatives, Dr. Means has shown that with the right tools and a heart full of compassion, even the most daunting health challenges can be overcome.

Dr. Casey Means' story as the Global Glucose Guardian is a vivid illustration of how one person's vision can ignite a global movement, transforming the landscape of public health and proving that innovation, guided by compassion, knows no boundaries. Her journey continues to inspire all who dream of a healthier world, making each step she takes a testament to the power of passion and perseverance in the face of global health challenges.

Chapter 11: Tomorrow's Medicine, Today

Visions of the future: Predictions and projects that promise to further revolutionize health care.

As the sun sets on today's healthcare landscape, Dr. Casey Means stands on the precipice of tomorrow, gazing into a future where technology and human insight merge to create revolutionary approaches to health and wellness. This chapter delves deep into the visionary projects and bold predictions that Dr. Means champions, illuminating her role as a pioneer at the forefront of tomorrow's medicine.

At the heart of Dr. Means' vision is the integration of artificial intelligence (AI) with personalized health monitoring systems. She envisions a world where AI doesn't just support healthcare professionals but becomes a proactive partner in managing individual health. These AI systems are designed to analyze vast amounts of health data in real-time, identifying patterns and predicting potential health issues before they become critical. Dr. Means often quotes Alan Kay's saying, "The best way to predict the future is to invent it," as she discusses her work in developing these predictive technologies.

One of the flagship projects that Dr. Means is spearheading is an advanced metabolic tracking system that combines genetic, environmental, and behavioral data to provide personalized health plans. This project, still in its pilot phase, has already shown promise in drastically reducing incidences of metabolic syndrome among participants. Dr. Means highlights the project's potential: "We are not just at the cusp of change but are actively forging a new paradigm where each individual can be the master of their health destiny."

Dr. Means also predicts a significant shift towards more holistic health measures in mainstream medicine. She advocates for a 'whole system' approach that considers every aspect of an individual's lifestyle, from diet and exercise to mental health and social interactions. This approach is exemplified in her collaboration with urban planners and architects to design 'health-positive' living spaces—environments that naturally encourage movement, community interaction, and accessibility to healthy food options.

Another revolutionary aspect of Dr. Means' work involves the democratization of health education. She is developing an open-source health education platform that utilizes machine learning to tailor content to the learning styles and needs of its users. This platform aims to empower individuals from all socioeconomic backgrounds to take charge of their health, breaking down barriers that have traditionally hindered access to health knowledge.

In response to the global challenge of aging populations, Dr. Means is also involved in a project that uses telemedicine to provide continuous care for the elderly. This service not only monitors health metrics but also uses predictive algorithms to recommend preventive measures, thereby enhancing the quality of life and reducing the need for hospitalization. Dr. Means sees this as a crucial step towards sustainable healthcare: "As our societies grow older, our approach to healthcare must evolve not just to extend life but to enhance the quality of those extra years."

Throughout the chapter, Dr. Means' insights into the future of medicine are interspersed with personal stories from those who have participated in her early projects, providing a human touch to her high-tech visions. These narratives reinforce her belief that technology should be a tool for enhancing human connection rather than replacing it.

As you turn the final pages of this chapter, you are not only educated about the possibilities of future medicine but are also inspired by Dr. Means' unwavering optimism and innovative spirit. Her vision of tomorrow's medicine, rooted in today's emerging technologies and guided by timeless principles of care and compassion, offers a hopeful outlook for a world in dire need of healing.

This chapter not only promises a future where medical care is more effective, personalized, and preventive but also motivates readers to imagine their role in this exciting new era of healthcare. Dr. Casey Means' narrative continues to serve as a powerful reminder that the future of health is not just a distant dream but a reality being shaped today.

Chapter 12: The Ripple Effect

Living Her Legacy: The Ongoing Impact of Dr. Means' Work on Future Generations

In the vast ocean of healthcare, Dr. Casey Means has cast stones that create ripples extending far beyond the initial splash. Her pioneering work in metabolic health, relentless advocacy for preventive medicine, and visionary integration of technology have not just transformed lives in the present—they are sculpting a healthier future for generations to come. This chapter explores the profound and enduring legacy of Dr. Means' work, demonstrating how her contributions are poised to resonate for decades.

Dr. Means' legacy is built on the foundation of empowerment—empowering individuals to take control of their health, empowering communities to foster wellness, and empowering a global audience to embrace preventive healthcare. Her approach combines cutting-edge technology with a compassionate touch, a synergy that magnifies her impact. As she often quotes from Margaret Mead, "Never doubt that a small group of thoughtful, committed citizens can change the world; indeed, it's the only thing that ever has." Dr. Means embodies this principle, showing that committed action can indeed reshape the world.

The ripple effects of her work are visible in various aspects of society. In education, Dr. Means has revolutionized how health literacy is approached. By developing curriculum integrations for schools that teach children the importance of nutrition, exercise, and mental well-being from an early age, she ensures that future generations grow up with the knowledge to make health-conscious decisions. These educational programs have already shown promising results, with participating schools reporting lower rates of childhood obesity and higher levels of student engagement in health-related activities.

In the realm of public health policy, Dr. Means has been instrumental in advocating for legislation that supports preventive care measures. Her efforts have led to increased funding for research into lifestyle-related diseases and the implementation of public health campaigns that promote active living and healthy eating. Her influence in policy-making demonstrates her belief in the power of systemic change, affirming that "health is not just an individual responsibility but a collective promise."

Dr. Means' legacy also extends to the global stage, where her initiatives in underserved communities have introduced sustainable health practices that are culturally sensitive and locally embraced. In parts of Africa and Asia, for example, the mobile clinics established through her foundation have not only provided necessary medical care but have also trained local healthcare workers, creating a self-sustaining model of health education and empowerment.

Moreover, Dr. Means' leadership in the tech industry continues to inspire a new generation of entrepreneurs, particularly women and minorities, to enter a field that has traditionally lacked diversity. Her mentorship programs and start-up incubators have been pivotal in breaking down barriers and fostering an environment where innovation thrives on the diversity of thought and experience.

As the chapter unfolds, it presents personal stories from individuals whose lives have been transformed by Dr. Means' work. From a young software developer who was inspired to create an app that helps users track mental health, to a community leader who now organizes local health fairs, the personal anecdotes serve as testimonials to the widespread impact of her legacy.

The closing pages of this chapter invite readers to reflect on their own potential to effect change. Dr. Means' story is a clarion call to action, urging each individual to consider how they can contribute to the health of their communities and the world at large. She reminds us that "each ripple we create can build a current strong enough to change the course of our collective future."

Through captivating narrative and inspirational quotes, this chapter not only chronicles the lasting impact of Dr. Casey Means' work but also imbues you with a sense of responsibility and hope. Her legacy is not encapsulated by the projects she has started or the policies she has influenced; it is ongoing, driven by every life touched and changed by her vision. Dr. Means' work is a testament to the power of one individual's efforts to ignite a global movement toward better health, proving that the ripple effects of true innovation can indeed be endless.

Made in United States
Orlando, FL
21 September 2024

51783453R00039